Guide to the Academic Dress of the University of Bath

https://www.burgon.org.uk/

Guide to the Academic Dress of the University of Bath

Edward Ripley

The Burgon Society

Copyright © The Burgon Society

The right of Edward Ripley to be identified as the author of this work has been asserted in accordance with the Copyright, Design and Patents Act, 1988.

First published 2022 in the United Kingdom (2)

The Burgon Society

https://www.burgon.org.uk

British Library Cataloguing in Publication Data

A CIP catalogue record for this book is available from the British Library

Library of Congress Cataloguing in Publication Data
Edward Ripley

For ISBN see rear cover

Brief history of the University

The University can trace its roots back to the Bristol Trade School, School of Applied Science, which was founded in 1865. The School itself was very successful, and later in the century became the Merchant Venturers' Technical College (MVTC), under the control of the society of Merchant Venturers. In 1909 the city's college was granted a charter to become the University of Bristol, at which point the MVTC provided the University with a faculty of Engineering. In 1929 MVTC took over control of the Bath School of Chemistry and Pharmacy, solidifying its links with the sciences.

However, it soon became apparent that it was no longer financially viable for the Merchant Venturers to continue to operate the College. Talks were subsequently entered into with Bristol City Council and Bristol University, the outcome being that the local authority would take over the management of the College, which was to be renamed Bristol College of Technology. (It was also at this point that the links with Bristol University were broken.)

In 1956 BCT was upgraded to the Regional College of the South West, which was further enhanced by becoming a College of Advanced Technology in 1959. At this point the college split into two: the Bristol College of Science and Technology (BCST), the predecessor of the University, and Bristol Technological College, a predecessor of UWE, both located on Ashley Down.

Following the Robbins Report of 1963, BCST sought to gain university status; however there was insufficient space at the site and no suitable alternative was available in Bristol. A chance encounter between the College's principal and the Director of Education for Bath at a children's school play in late 1963 resulted in the offer of a site just outside Bath; this would later be formalised to a site of 150 acres. The College therefore assumed the title of Bath University of Technology, receiving its Royal Charter in 1966, later changing in 1971 to The University of Bath.

Initial designs for academic dress

The thought process for the initial designs of both hoods and gowns can be pieced together through surviving letters between the University, academic dress scholar Dr G. W. Shaw and the robe-makers Ede and Ravenscroft. These are considered in turn in the *Transactions of the Burgon Society* article, 'Academic Dress of the University of Bath 1966-2020'; however what can be summarised for the purposes of this booklet is that the designs were simple and on the whole remain the same to the present. They have adapted well to additional degrees being added, using the addition of coloured ribbons applied to the hood.

> *The basic hood material is old gold grosgrain, symbolising the colour of Bath stone, and degrees are distinguished by the colours of the linings. The scheme is very simple, there being only four hoods without the complicated distinctions for various disciplines which seem to proliferate these days.*

> Dr A. W. Hardie (Vice Principal of BCST) 1965

Above are the four hoods that Dr Hardie mentions. All hoods have the University colour of old-gold, which is representative of the Bath stone. The lining and neck bands are a different colour to represent the level of the award.

The hoods themselves are in the Leeds shape [s7]; the cowl edge is permanently turned out by 2″ which leads through to the neck band, which is a V shape, making the taffeta lining visible.

It should be noted that the official regulations throughout the University's history has called these Oxford simple shape [s1], though this is incorrect as there would not be a fixed turn-out or a neck band in a V shape. The Leeds hood is based on the Oxford simple shape.

These hoods remain in use at the University and have been further differentiated by the additions of grosgrain ribbon, of 1″ width, applied to the turn-out, though these all are a later addition to the original designs.

In the following account, the University's regulations are in italics.

Academic Dress Regulations

General Provisions

When wearing academic dress, members of the University, including graduating students, should wear a dark suit, trousers, or skirt, with a collared white shirt or blouse. If a shirt is worn this should be fastened at the neck with a tie. Dark shoes should be worn. Alternatively, traditional national costume or services uniform may be worn.

Foundation Degree

A gown of black stuff of the basic bachelors' shape [b1]. The gown has a gathered yoke at the back and open sleeves that are pointed at the bottom. The gown should be mid-calf to ankle in length. The hood is a Leeds shape [s7] and is made of old-gold grosgrain and is lined with old-gold taffeta. It is the only Bath hood that is monochromatic.

Headwear is a square cap [h1], also known as a mortarboard, made of black cloth.

The Foundation degree was introduced in 2006.

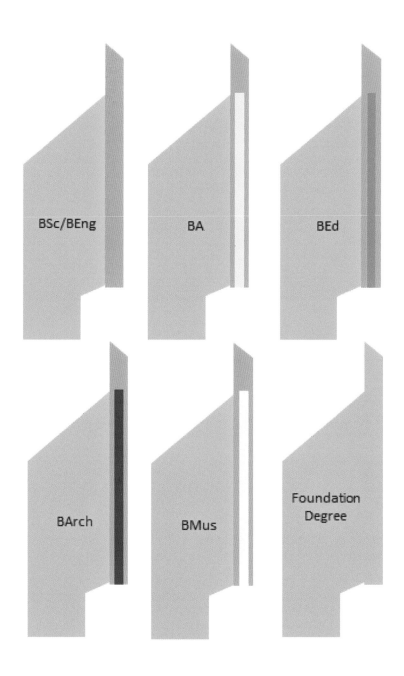

Foundation and Bachelors' Degree Hoods

Bachelors' Degrees

A gown of black stuff of the basic bachelors' shape [b1]. The gown has a gathered yoke at the back and open sleeves that are pointed at the bottom. The gown should be mid-calf to ankle in length. The hood is a Leeds shape [s7] and is made of old-gold grosgrain and is lined with olive-green taffeta. Ribbons are applied as follows:

Bachelor of Science (BSc) and Bachelor of Engineering (BEng), has no ribbon applied, introduced in 1966

Bachelor of Arts (BA), has a 1" ribbon of pale yellow applied to the turn out, introduced by 1971

Bachelor of Education (BEd), has a 1" ribbon of orange applied to the turn out, introduced by 1971

Bachelor of Architecture (BArch), has a 1" ribbon of mid crimson applied to the turn out, introduced by 1971

Bachelor of Music (BMus), has a 1" ribbon of cream damask* applied to the turn out, introduced in 1992

Headwear shall be a square cap [h1], also known as a mortarboard made of black cloth.

*There are a wide variety of cream damasks used in the production of academic dress; however, given the design similarities with Oxford, it can be assumed that apple blossom damask is the most likely choice.

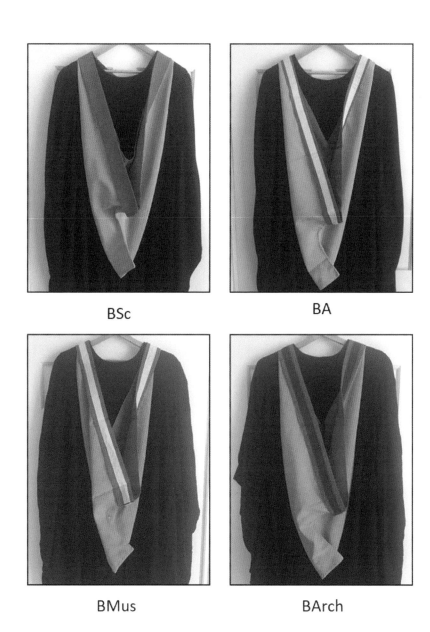

BSc

BA

BMus

BArch

Examples of Bachelors' Hoods
Private Collection

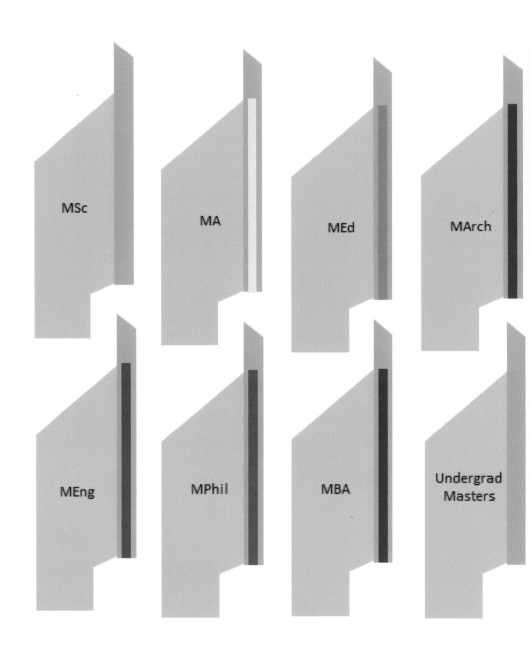

MSc

MA

MEd

MArch

MEng

MPhil

MBA

Undergrad
Masters

Undergraduate Masters' and Masters' Degree Hoods

Undergraduate Masters' (First Degree Masters') Degree

A gown of black stuff of the Cambridge MA shape [m2]. The gown has a gathered yoke at the back and closed sleeves with an opening at elbow height. The sleeves extend to the bottom of the gown with a shallow crescent shape cut out on the back edge. The hood is a Leeds shape [s7] and is made of old-gold grosgrain and is lined with pale blue taffeta, with an olive-green ribbon of 1" width applied to the turn out.

Headwear shall be a square cap [h1], also known as a mortarboard made of black cloth.

The undergraduate masters degree was introduced in 2001, following a review of what constitutes a masters level degree. The University's MEng, MArch and MPharm courses were given the status of undergraduate masters with the addition of the following courses: MBiochem; MBiol; MChem; MMath; MPharmacol; and MPhys. The University still retains the MArch and MEng hoods in its regulations; these can still be awarded for postgraduate study or as honorary degrees (*honoris causa*).

Masters' degrees

A gown of black stuff of the Cambridge MA shape [m2]. The gown has a gathered yoke at the back and closed sleeves with an opening at elbow height; the sleeves extend to the bottom of the gown with a shallow crescent shape cut out on the back edge. The hood is a Leeds shape [s7] and is made of old-gold grosgrain and is lined with pale blue taffeta. Ribbons are applied as follows:

Master of Science (MSc); Master of Pharmacy (MPharm) and Master of Research (MRes), has no ribbon. This was introduced in 1966. For a brief period (2006-2008) the MRes degree had its own hood with a 1" old-gold ribbon applied to the turn out.

Master of Arts (MA), has a 1" ribbon of pale yellow applied to the turn out, introduced by 1971.

Master of Education (MEd), has a 1" ribbon of orange applied to the turn out, introduced by 1971.

Master of Architecture (MArch), has a 1" ribbon of mid-crimson applied to the turn out, introduced by 1971.

Master of Engineering (MEng), has a 1" ribbon of purple applied to the turn out, introduced in 1980.

Master of Philosophy (MPhil), has a 1" ribbon of red applied to the turn out, introduced in 1984.

Master of Business Administration (MBA), has a 1" ribbon of dark blue applied to the turn out, introduced in 1987.

Master of Surgery (MSurg), see comments in professional doctorates.

Headwear is a square cap [h1], also known as a mortarboard made of black cloth.

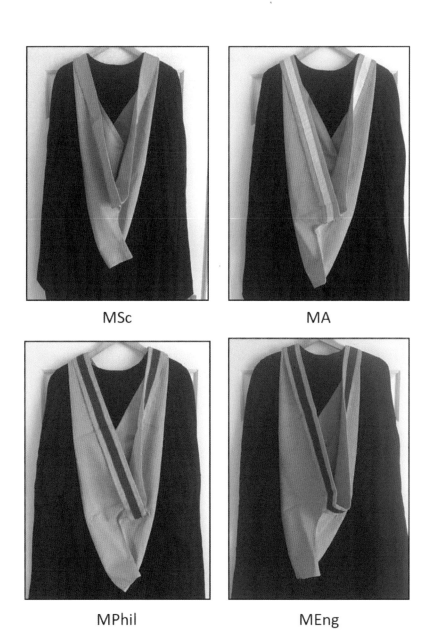

MSc   MA

MPhil   MEng

Examples of Masters' Hoods

Private Collection

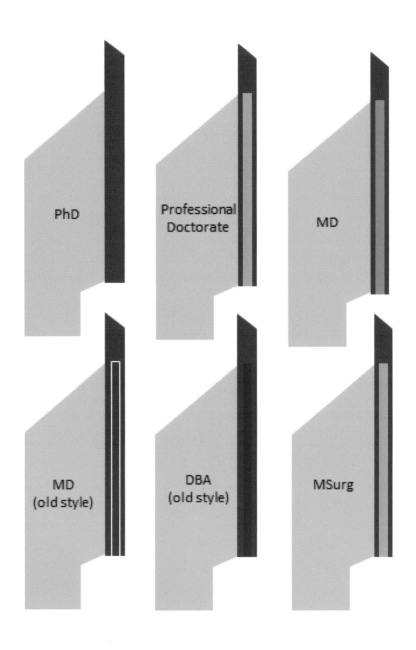

Taught and Professional Doctorate Hoods (incl MSurg)

Professional and Taught Doctorates

A gown of medium crimson cloth of the Oxford doctors' shape [d2]. The gown has a gathered yoke at the back and open bell-shaped sleeves that end at the wrist. There are old-gold grosgrain facings of 5" applied at the front of the gown and the sleeves also have facings of 9" applied from the cuff upwards. To differentiate between degrees, 1" ribbon is applied to the outer edgings of the facings and to the upper edges of the cuff facings. The hood is a Leeds shape [s7] and is made of old-gold grosgrain and is lined with medium crimson taffeta, ribbons are applied as follows.

Doctor of Philosophy (PhD), has no ribbon applied. This was introduced in 1966.

Professional Doctorates were introduced in 1998 and include the Doctor of Education (EdD); Doctor of Engineering (EngD); Doctor of Business Administration (DBA); Doctor of Health (DHealth); Doctor of Policy Research and Practice (DPRP); and Doctor of Clinical Psychology (DClinPsyc) has a ribbon of 1" olive-green applied to their hoods and gowns.

Initially the above design was for the EdD; the DBA had a unique gown with dark blue edging, introduced in 2005: the other professional doctorate degrees hadn't been introduced at that point. However, in 2008 the EdD gown became the professional doctorate gown and the DBA design was abolished (though those who were awarded it 2005-2008 can continue to wear it).

Doctor of Medicine (MD) has a 1" ribbon of pink applied to the gown and hood, introduced by 2007. Initially this had a crimson ribbon applied, and was changed in 2008.

Master of Surgery (MSurg); has a 1″ ribbon of pale blue applied to the gown and hood, introduced by 2007.

Headwear is a black velvet bonnet [h2] with a silver tassel

PhD Gown and Hood
Private Collection

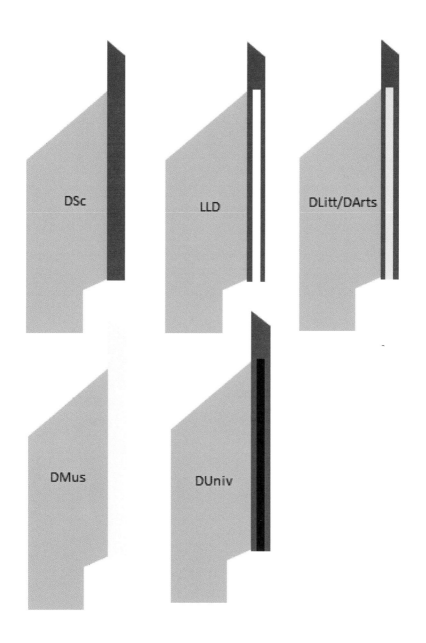

Higher Doctorate Hoods

Higher Doctorates

A gown of scarlet cloth of the Oxford doctors' shape [d2]. The gown has a gathered yoke at the back and open bell-shaped sleeves that end at the wrist. There are old-gold grosgrain facings of 5" applied at the front of the gown and the sleeves also have facings of 9" applied from the cuff upwards. To differentiate between degrees, 1" ribbon is applied to the outer edgings of the facings and to the upper edges of the cuff facings. The hood is a Leeds shape [s7] and is made of old-gold grosgrain and is lined with scarlet taffeta, ribbons are applied as follows.

Doctor of Science (DSc) and Doctor of Engineering *honoris causa* (DEng), has no ribbon applied, introduced in 1966.

Doctor of Law (LLD), has a 1" white ribbon applied to the gown and hood. This was introduced in 1966.

Doctor of Letters (DLitt) and Doctor of Arts (DArt), has a 1" yellow ribbon applied to the gown and hood, introduced in 1970 for the DLitt, and 1998 for the DArt.

Doctor of the University (DUniv), has a 1" black ribbon applied to the good and gown, introduced in 2018

Doctor of Music (DMus), has cream damask replacing the scarlet cloth and taffeta, on the hood and gown, there are no ribbons applied, introduced in 1992.

Headwear is a black velvet bonnet [h2] with a gold tassel

Doctor of Music Gown and Hood
(in apple blossom damask)
Private Collection

Doctor of Science Gown and Hood
University of Bath

Bath Specific Gowns

There was a point in the University's history where it had specific gowns for the bachelors' and masters' awards. However, these proved to be short-lived, being removed from the specifications in 1997, and replaced with the current guidelines.

The initial designs for gowns at the University were that they would all be the same, regardless of level of degree. The rationale was that one gown looked much the same as another at a distance. The development of these is charted in 'Academic Dress of the University of Bath 1966-2020': they were the design of Dr G. W. Shaw.

The Bath bachelors' gown [b7] was to be based on the Oxford bachelors' gown with a 6" slit above the arm hole with a black stuff-covered button at the top of the slit.

The Bath masters' gown [m16] was based on a standard masters' gown, but with a square bottomed sleeve with an oblique cut at a 45° angle on the front-facing corner. The sleeve would have a 6" slit, leading to the armhole being an inverted T shape, with a black stuff covered button at the top.

The Bath doctoral undress gown would be that of the masters gown with the addition of Cambridge doctoral lace around the armhole. Interestingly this still remains in the regulations; however, given the likelihood of actual usage at the University it can also be considered defunct.

Officers' Robes

The Chancellor's official dress shall be a robe of black all-silk satin damask with 3" wide gold lace facings and gold ornamentation; a black velvet square cap [h1] trimmed with gold lace and gold bullion button and tassel.

The Pro-Chancellor's official dress shall be a robe of black all-silk satin damask with 1" wide gold lace facings and gold ornamentation; a black velvet square cap [h1] with gold bullion button and tassel.

The Vice-Chancellor's The official dress shall be a robe of black all-silk satin damask with 1¾" wide gold lace facings and gold ornamentation; a black velvet square cap [h1] trimmed with gold lace and gold button with gold tassel.

The Deputy Vice-Chancellor's The official dress shall be a robe of black silk ottoman with ½" wide gold lace; a black velvet mortarboard [h1] with gold button and black tassel.

The Treasurer's official dress shall be a robe of black silk ottoman trimmed with 1⅝" wide gold lace; a black velvet square cap [h1] with gold button and black tassel.

The Pro-Vice-Chancellor's official dress shall be a robe of black silk ottoman with ½" wide gold lace; a black velvet square cap [h1] with gold button and black tassel.

The Marshal's official dress shall be a gown of black stuff of traditional Master shape; facings and yoke trimmed with 1" gold ribbon; a black cloth square cap [h1] trimmed with gold ribbon and gold button with gold tassel.

The Chair of Council's official dress shall be a robe of black silk ottoman, trimmed with 1" wide gold lace; a black square cap [h1] with black button and gold tassel.

The Bedell's official dress shall be a robe of dark blue cloth, trimmed with ½" gold lace, with a dark blue cloth bonnet [h2] with a gold cord and tassel.

Chancellor's Cap
University of Bath

Chancellor's Gown
University of Bath

L: Vice Chancellor's Gown
R: Deputy Vice Chancellor or Pro-Vice Chancellor's Gown
University of Bath

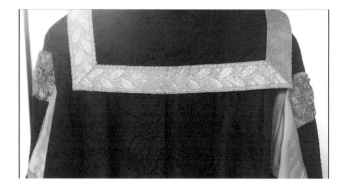

Detail of the back of the Vice Chancellor's Gown
University of Bath

Honorary degrees

Honorary degrees are awarded by the University for those who have demonstrated superior merit in their field of expertise nationally or internationally.

The award of these degrees, *honoris causa*, occurs during the graduation ceremonies itself each year. These awards have created some interesting quirks within the University's academic dress which are outlined below.

The awards of LLD, DLitt and DMus are unusual in that the University does not teach these subjects itself, however, but does award them *honoris causa*. The degrees themselves are standard higher doctorate degrees in British institutions, in most cases the designs were settled out of necessity of the University wishing to grant an honorary degree. For example, the DMus and BMus awards were first introduced in 1992, with the first DMus award in 1993 to Amelia Freedman MBE FRAM, for her work with Bath International Festival, for which she was director from 1986 to 1993. Interestingly a BMus has never been awarded.

Another quirk appears in the honorary DEng being given a different gown to the taught/professional EngD. This degree has a DSc gown and hood rather than the professional doctorate gown and hood. It can be assumed that holders of the DEng were awarded a DSc. Given the strong links with engineering at the institution and that the first record of an honorary degree was in 2000. This would also help to explain why it shares the DSc, and doesn't use the professional doctorate gown and hood, which is retained for the other professional doctorates when awarded *honoris causa*.

Up to 2020 the University has awarded 558 honorary degrees: it is unsurprising that the proportion of DSc awards is the highest.

Doctor of Law Gown and Hood (p18)
University of Bath

N.B the ribbon is applied incorrectly to the interior of the hood, suggesting along with the date of the label, pre 1969 that this was one of the first LLDs to be produced and may have been a prototype.

Abbreviations for degrees

BA/MA/DArts	Bachelor/Master/Doctor of Arts
BArch/MArch	Bachelor/Master of Architecture
BEd/MEd/EdD	Bachelor/Master/Doctor of Education
BEng/MEng/DEng	Bachelor/Master/Doctor of Engineering
BMus/DMus	Bachelor/Doctor of Music
BPharm/MPharm	Bachelor/Master of Pharmacy
BSc/MSc/DSc	Bachelor/Master/Doctor of Science
DClinPsyc	Doctor of Clinical Psychology
DHealth	Doctor of Health
DLitt	Doctor of Letters
DPRP	Doctor of Public Research and Policy
DUniv	Doctor of the University
LLD	Doctor of Law
MBA/DBA	Master/Doctor of Business Administration
MBioChem	Master of Biochemistry
MBiol	Master of Biology
MChem	Master of Chemistry
MD	Doctor of Medicine
MMath	Master of Mathematics
MPharmacol	Master of Pharmacology
MPhil/PhD	Master/Doctor of Philosophy
MPhys	Master of Physics
MSurg	Master of Surgery

About the author:

About the Author: Edward Ripley was awarded a BSc from the University of Bath and has recently been admitted to Fellowship to the Burgon Society for his work on the 'Academic Dress of the University of Bath 1966-2020'. He is a Chartered Accountant, holding membership to the Institute for Chartered Accountants for England and Wales (ICAEW).

Information included in this guide is from the University of Bath's official regulations for academic dress.

References in square brackets refer to the Grove's classification system of academical dress.

The Burgon Society is the national organization dedicated to the study of academic dress. More information can be found on its website (burgon.org.uk).
The Society is a charity registered in England & Wales, number 1137522.

Membership of the Society is open to anybody who is interested in academic dress. Annual subscription entitles Members and Fellows to a free copy of our annual peer-reviewed journal, *Transactions of the Burgon Society*, on publication, as well as our quarterly newsletter *Burgon Notes*. Members can also access discounts for events and in the Society's shop. Members can also apply for Fellowship of the Society by examination.

Contact secretary@burgon.org.uk

Printed in Great Britain
by Amazon

76883311R00018